Published by
CHARTWELL BOOKS, INC.
A Division of BOOK SALES, INC.
110 Enterprise Avenue
Secaucus, New Jersey 07094
Printed in Italy
SBN 0-89009-733-X

the children's
picture dictionary

Text by Brenda Apsley
Illustrations by Jane Cunningham

CHARTWELL
BOOKS, INC.

a A

above

The bird is **above** the cat.

The cat is **above** the dog.

add

Add 2 and 3. The answer is 5.

against

The ladder leans **against** the wall.

The bike leans **against** the fence

accident

David did not mean to break the jug.

It was an **accident**.

address

JOHN SMITH
10 HIGH ST
CHEADLE
CHESHIRE
SK8 1AL

Where you live is your **address**.

air

Air is all around us

We breathe **air**.

We blow **air** into balloons.

acorn

An **acorn** is the fruit of the oak tree.

aeroplane

An **aeroplane** is a machine that flies.

airport

Aeroplanes land and take off at the **airport**.

across

The children walk **across** the crossing.

Passengers catch aeroplanes from the **airport**.

alike

The twins look the same.
They are **alike.**

The dogs are very different.
They are not **alike.**

alphabet

a b c d
e f g h
i j k l
m n o p
q r s t u
v w x y z

The letters of the **alphabet** make words.

There are 26 letters in the **alphabet.**

animal

Animals come in all shapes, sizes and colours.

A fish is an **animal.**

A cow is an **animal.**

mouse

lion

elephant

horse

bear

frog

snake

spider

parrot

bat

giraffe

all

All the flowers are red.

always

Always means every time, at all times.

Coal is **always** black.

Snow is **always** white.

alone

Susan is on her own.
She is **alone.**

and

And is a joining word.

Eggs **and** bacon.

Knife **and** fork.

Cup **and** saucer.

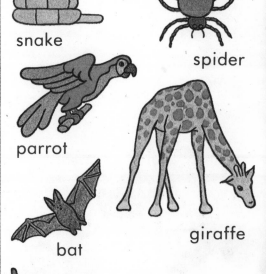

octopus

pig

along

The cat walks **along** the wall.
So does David.

angry

Susan is **angry.**

Here are more **angry** words: cross, furious.

Anything that lives and is not a plant is an **animal.**

ankle

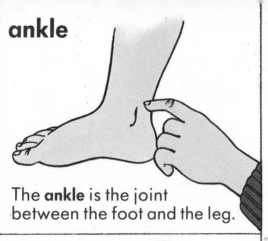

The **ankle** is the joint between the foot and the leg.

arm

The boy has two **arms**.

So does the chair.

So does the monkey.

asleep

The baby is not awake.
The baby is **asleep**.

answer

The teacher asks a question.

David knows the **answer**.

Dad hurries to **answer** the telephone.

astronaut

An **astronaut** travels through space in a spaceship.

arrow

An **arrow** is a pointed stick shot from a bow.

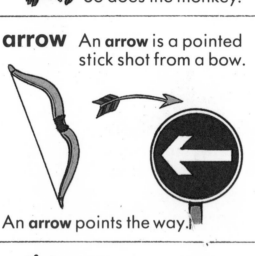

An **arrow** points the way.

aunt

Daddy's sister is my **aunt**.
Mummy's sister is my **aunt**.

ant

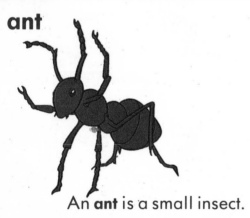

An **ant** is a small insect.

artist

An **artist** is a person who paints or draws.

autumn

A year has four seasons.

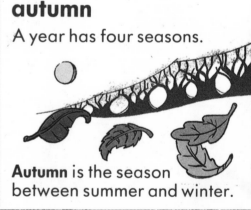

Autumn is the season between summer and winter.

apple

An **apple** is a fruit.

Apples grow on trees.

ask

WHAT TIME IS IT?

David **asks** a question.

awake

The baby is not asleep.
The baby is **awake**.

b B

aby

baby is a very young child.

bake

To **bake** is to cook in the oven.
Mum has **baked** a cake.

bank

A **bank** is a place
to keep money in.

ack

he children are standing
ack to **back**.

usan takes her book
ack to the library.

ball

We play games with round **balls**.
The boy throws the **ball**.

bat We play games with **bats**.

The boy will hit the ball
with his **bat**.

balloon

Blow into the **balloon**
to fill it with air.

beach

The **beach** is the sandy
area by the sea.

ad
Sam is a **bad** dog.

Anything not good is **bad**.
he apple is **bad**.

band

A **band** is people
who play music together.

beak

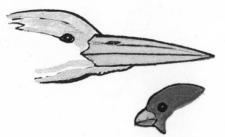

Birds eat with their **beaks.**

between

Daddy is sitting **between** the children.
Between means in the middle of.

bird

A **bird** is an animal with wings and feathers. Most **birds** can fly.

sparrow

robin

pigeon

duck

penguin

turkey

toucan

ostrich

owl

hummingbird

eagle

gull

peacock

bed

We sleep in a **bed.**
Spot has his own **bed.**

bicycle

A **bicycle** has two wheels.
Can you ride a **bicycle**?

bee

A **bee** is a black and yellow flying insect.
Bees make honey.

big

Big means large.
The red truck is **big**.

bell

Bells ring.
Bells come in all shapes and sizes.

bigger

The blue truck is **bigger**.

belt

Ben and Bob both have brown **belts.**

biggest

The yellow truck is the **biggest**.

birthday

Today is John's fifth **birthday**.
He was born five years ago.

blanket

A **blanket** is a warm cover.
This **blanket** is blue.

book

Books have words and pictures.
Do you like reading **books**?

biscuit

Biscuits are sweet things to eat.

blow

The wind **blows**.
John **blows** his horn.

both

Both the girls have umbrellas.
Both the umbrellas have spots.

bite

The boy **bites** into his apple.

blue

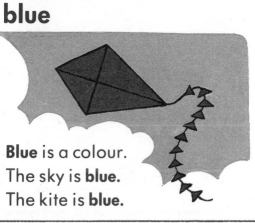

Blue is a colour.
The sky is **blue**.
The kite is **blue**.

bottom

Jack is at the **bottom**
of the hill.
Jill is at the top.

black

The coal is **black**.
The cat is **black**.

boat

We ride on water in a **boat**.
Boats come in all
shapes and sizes.

box

This **box** holds
breakfast cereal.

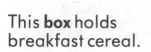

This **box** holds
chocolates.
What other things
come in **boxes**?

blackboard

The teacher writes
on the **blackboard**.

bread

Bread is good to eat.
The baker bakes **bread**.

breakfast

Breakfast is the meal we eat in the morning.
Susan is having a boiled egg for **breakfast**.

bubble

A **bubble** is round and filled with air.
Bubbles burst when you touch them.

James is blowing **bubbles**.

busy

Busy people have lots to do

brick

Bricks are hard.
Many buildings are made of **brick**.

build

Build means to make something.
The **builder builds** a house.

Buildings come in all shapes and sizes.

church

skyscraper

house

school

cinema

factory

butter

Butter is a food.
Butter tastes good on bread.

butterfly

A **butterfly** is an insect with four wings.

bridge

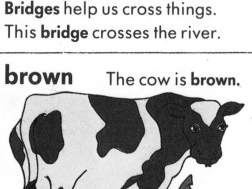

Bridges help us cross things.
This **bridge** crosses the river.

brown

The cow is **brown.**

The log is **brown.**

button

Buttons fasten John's coat.
The **buttons** are blue.

brush

Susan **brushes** her hair.

David **brushes** his teeth with a tooth **brush.**

bus

A **bus** carries many people. It is like a large car.

Do you go to school on a **bus**?

buy

Bob **buys** a boat.

Buy means to get something by paying money for it.

c C

age

The hamster
lives in
cage.
The canary
lives in a
cage, too.

can

I **can** ride a bike.
I am able to ride a bike.

Cans hold things.

carpet

The **carpet** covers the floor.

ake

Susan has baked a **cake**.
akes are good to eat.

candle

A **candle** burns
to give light.

Mary is putting **candles** on the cake.

carry

When you **carry** something
you take it from one place
to another.
Tim **carries** his case and book.

alendar

A **calendar** is a list
of all the days and dates
and months in a year.

SUN	MON	TUE	WED	THR	FRI	SAT
	1	2	3	4	5	6
7	8	9	10	11	12	13
14	15	16	17	18	19	20
21	22	23	24	25	26	27
28	29	30	31			

What
ate
oes the **calendar** show?

car

A **car** is a machine that moves.
A **car** takes us from
place to place.

castle

Castles were built long ago.
They had many rooms, and thick
walls to keep out the enemy.

camera

A **camera** is a machine
hat takes photographs.

careful

Sch__

Be **careful** when
you cross the road

This **castle** is made of sand

cat

A **cat** is a small, furry animal.
This **cat** is chasing leaves.

catch

The cat is trying to
catch the leaves.

The gardener is trying to
catch the cat.

caterpillar

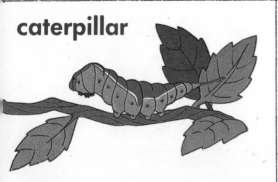

A **caterpillar** is a grub which
turns into a butterfly or moth.

chair

We sit on **chairs.**

cheese

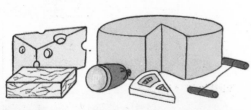

Cheese is a food made from milk.
here are many different
ds of **cheese.**

chest

The **chest** is the front part
of the body between the neck
and the waist.
This is another kind of **chest** —
a toy **chest**, or box.

child

A **child** is a young boy or girl.

Christmas

Christmas is the
birthday of Jesus.

Christmas comes every
year on December 25th.

Let's decorate the
Christmas tree.

church

A **church** is a place
where people go to pray.

circle

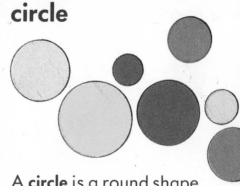

A **circle** is a round shape,
a ring.

circus

A **circus** is a special show.

acrobats

animal

clowns

city

A **city** is a ve
large to

Many people live and work
in a **city.**

assroom

A **classroom** is a room in a hool where children learn.

ean

Tom's face is **clean**. He's just washed it.

m's face isn't **clean**. s dirty.

imb

e child is **climbing** the stairs. ants **climb**, too.

ock

A **clock** shows us what time it is.

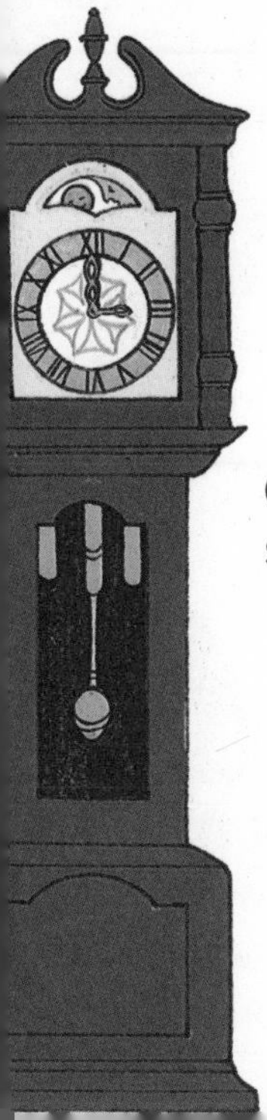

Clocks come in all shapes and sizes.

clothes

Clothes are things to wear.

pyjamas

dress

jacket

shirt

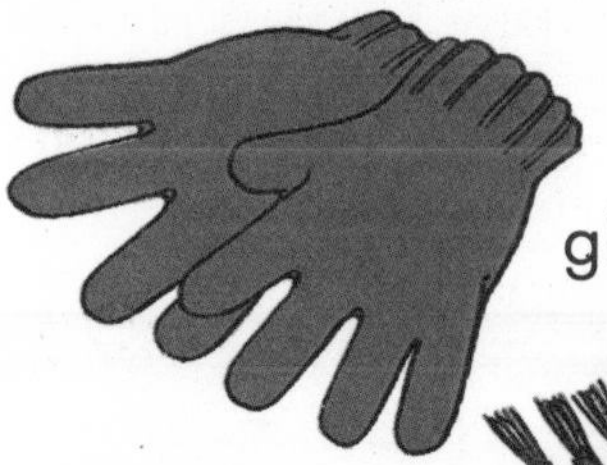

gloves

skirt

scarf

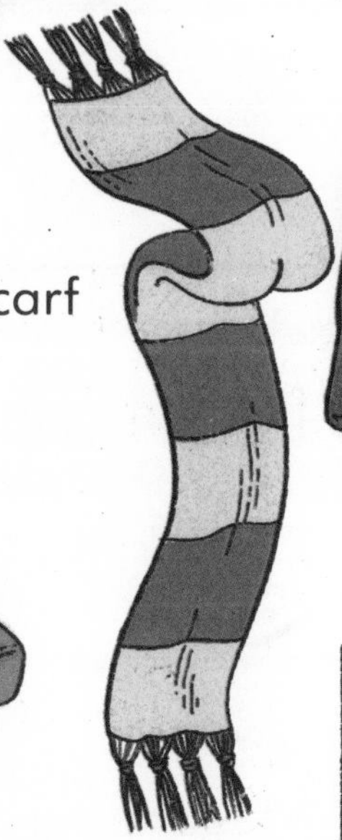

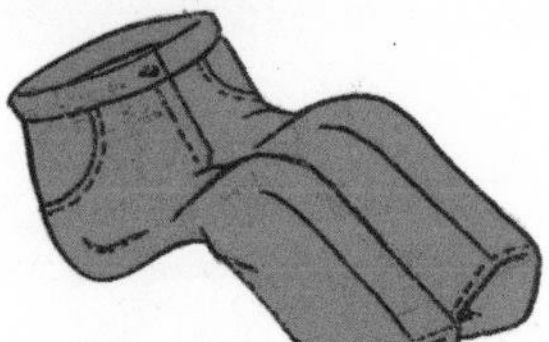

trousers

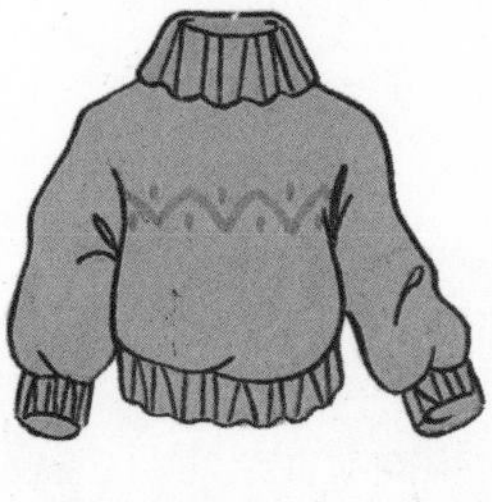

jumper

t-shirt

cloud

Clouds in the sky are white in good weather.

Clouds are dark in bad weather.

clown

Clowns have funny faces.

Clowns make us laugh.

coal

We burn **coal** for heat.

Coal is dug out of the ground.

coat

A **coat** keeps us warm.

Sheep have **coats**, too. Their woolly **coat** is called a fleece.

cobweb

A **cobweb** is a fine net made by a spider to catch insects in.

coffee

Coffee is a drink.

Do you like **coffee**?

comb

A **comb** is used for tidying hair.
We **comb** our hair.

crawl

The boy **crawls** under the table

Insects **crawl** too

cold

Cold is not hot.

Ice is **cold**.

Snow is **cold**.

Jane has a **cold**.
She is coughing and sneezing.

cook

Mummy makes lunch.
She **cooks** it.

This man
is a **cook**.

count

David is **counting** his money.
He is finding out how
much he has.

Can you **count**?

1 2 3 4 5 6 7 8 9 10

Count from 1 to 10.

cry

When James hurt his knee
he started to **cry**.

A **cry** is a loud shout, too.

cup

We drink from a **cup**.

The team won a silver **cup**.

colours

Everything has a **colour**.

The **colour** of the flower is pink.

The **colour** of the grass is green.

What **colour** is the ball?

cover

To **cover** means to put one
thing over another.
The blanket **covers**
the baby.

The book has a blue **cover**.

curtain

Curtains cover the window.
Curtains keep out light.

cut

Jane **cut** out a
paper doll.

Jane **cut** her finger
on the scissors

d D

ance

...cy is learning to **dance**.

day A **day** is the time from morning till night.

It is light during the **day**.

dentist

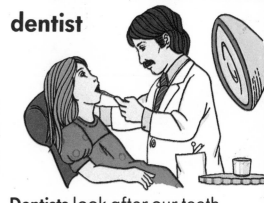

Dentists look after our teeth.

anger

danger
...gn means
...ok out' or 'be careful'.

decide

Tim can't **decide** which t-shirt to have.

He can't make up his mind.

Susan can't **decide** which cake to choose.

She can't make up her mind.

describe To **describe** means to tell more about.

Can you **describe** the dress?
The dress is blue.
The dress has short sleeves.
The dress has a pink belt.
The dress has two pockets.
The dress has a white collar.

ark It is **dark** at night.

...ark means without light.

ate The **date** is what day, month and year it is.

date is a sweet fruit.

deep The cave is **deep**.

The sea is **deep**, but the pool is not **deep**.

Deep means how far in or down something goes.

desert A **desert** is a large, dry, sandy area.

People ride camels in the **desert**.

desk

A **desk** is a table where we read, write and draw.

dig

Daddy **digs** in the garden. He turns the soil over.

dog

A **dog** is an anima with four legs.

Dogs are often kept as pets.

boxer

bulldog

dachshund

spaniel

dictionary

A **dictionary** is a book that lists words and what they mean. This book is a **dictionary**.

dirty

Daniel is digging too.

He is very **dirty**. He is not clean.

greyhound

Great Dane

poodle

different

Different means not the same.

The ducks are **different**. They are not the same.

The cars are all **different**. They are not the same.

How many **different** toys do you have?

dive

The boy is going to **dive** into the water.

divide

To **divide** means to split into parts, or to share.

Some **dogs** work.

husky

sheepdog

Mummy **divides** the pie into three pieces.

difficult

Difficult means not easy. **Difficult** means hard.

David thinks the sum is **difficult**. It is hard to do.

doctor

A **doctor** helps make sick people well.

These people are waiting to see the **doctor**.

doll A **doll** is a toy.

hese **dolls** are in **dolls'** house.

draw Dennis likes to **draw**. What has Dennis **drawn**?

drive The man **drives** a bus.

The woman **drives** a car.

donkey

A **donkey** ooks like small horse with big ears.

drawer A **drawer** is a place to keep things in.

How many **drawers** does this chest have?

drop A **drop** is a small amount of liquid.

Drops of rain are falling.

The boy has **dropped** his glove. He has let it fall.

door We go in and out through **doors**.

One **door** is open, ut the other **door** is closed.

dream

A **dream** is the pictures and thoughts in our minds as we sleep.

James **dreamed** he met a pink elephant.

David **dreamed** he was a king.

In Lucy's **dream** she was as small as a mouse.

drum

A **drum** is a musical instrument. We beat the **drum** with sticks.

down

ames is walking **down** the street.

dry The wind will blow the washing **dry**.

David's hands are wet. He **dries** them with a towel.

downstairs

ames is walking down the stairs. e is going **downstairs**.

drink

Can I have a **drink** of milk, please?

dust **Dust** is very tiny bits of dirt.

Diana **dusts** the furniture. She uses a **duster**.

e E

ear

The **ear** is what we hear sound with.

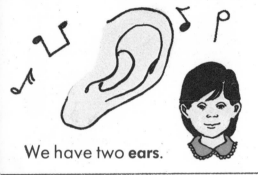

We have two **ears**.

easy

Easy means not hard, not difficult.

The jigsaw puzzle is **easy** to do. It's simple.

egg

Baby birds are born from **eggs**. We eat chicken and duck **eggs**.

We eat chocolate Easter **eggs**, too.

early

The train is **early**. It is ahead of time.

Try to be **early**. Try not to be late.

eat

Eat means to bite, chew and swallow food.

The children are **eating** hamburgers.

eight

Eight tells us how many.

Eight eggs.

1   2 3 4 5 6 7

earth

Our world is called the **earth**. We live on the planet **earth**.

Earth is soil.

Flowers, trees and plants grow in **earth**.

echo

An **echo** is a sound which bounces back.

Listen for the **echo** of your voice in a cave, tunnel or empty building.

edge

The knife blade has a sharp **edge**.

The vase is on the **edge** of the table.

elbow

The **elbow** is the part of the arm that bends.

electricity

Electricity is the power used to make light and heat.

Electricity drives machines, too.

elephant

The **elephant** is the largest
four-footed animal in the world.
Elephants have long trunks.

engine

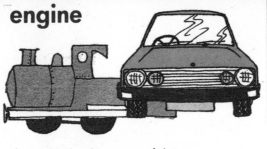

An **engine** is a machine.
The **engine** in a car makes it go.
The **engine** pulls the train.

evening

Evening is the last part
of the day.
After **evening** comes night.

eleven

Eleven tells us
how many.

Eleven elephants.

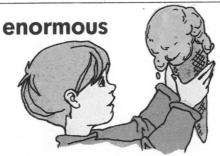

1
2
3
4
5
6
7
8
9
10
11

enormous

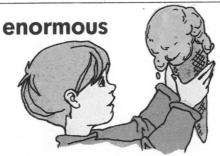

Enormous means very large.
Eric is eating an **enormous**
icecream.

enough

Enough means as
much as is needed.
Jane has
enough money
to buy the teddy.

every

We wake up **every**
morning.

We wash **every**
morning.

We eat breakfast **every** morning.

empty

Jane's purse is **empty**.
There is nothing in it.

envelope

We put letters in **envelopes**
before posting them.

exit

EXIT

Exit means way out.

end

Jim is at one **end**
of the rope.

John is at the
other **end**.

end also means to stop or finish.

escalator

An **escalator** is
a moving
stairway.

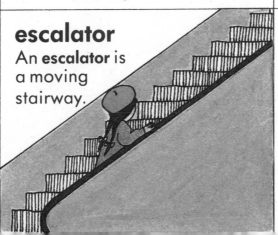

eye

The **eye** is the part of the
body used for seeing.
We see with our **eyes**.

f F

face

The **face** is the front part of the head.

The eyes, nose and mouth are part of the **face**.

fall

In autumn the leaves **fall** from the trees.

fasten

Fasten means to join together or lock.

Daddy **fastens** his seat belt.

fact

A **fact** is something that is true.

It is a **fact** that Bob has black hair.

family

Mummy, Daddy and the children are a **family**.

Aunts, uncles and cousins are part of the **family**, too.

fat

All the pigs are **fat**. They are large and round.

One pig is **fatter** than the others.

factory

A **factory** is a place where things are made.

farm

A **farm** is a place where crops are grown, and animals are kept.

feel

Feel the cat's fur. Does it **feel** silky?

fail

To **fail** is to be unable to do something.

The dog **failed** to catch the cat.

farmer

The **farmer** looks after the farm.

fence

The **fence** keeps the cows in the field.

Does your garden have a **fence**

ew

ew means not many.
...red only has a **few** marbles.

finger

Fingers are part of the hand.
Which **finger** has a ring on it?

fish A **fish** is an animal
that lives in water.

cod

eel

goldfish

salmon

plaice

seahorse

swordfish

shark

ield

A **field** is a piece of land.
Corn is growing in the **field**.

finish

Daddy **finished** the story.
He read it to the end.

ight

The children are **fighting**.
They both want the ball.

fire A **fire** burns.
We put coal on the **fire**.

Fires can be dangerous.

The **fire engine**
carries the **firemen**.
The **fireman** helps
to put out **fires**.

ill David has **filled** his glass
with milk.

...here is no room for any more.
...he glass is **full**.

fit

The shoe is
a good **fit**.

It's not too big
and not too small!

ind

...usan is trying to **find** her doll.
...an you see it?

first

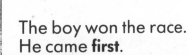

The boy won the race.
He came **first**.

five **Five** tells us how many.

1
2
3
4
5

Five foxes.

flag

Every country has its own **flag**.
The **flag** is the sign
of the country.

flat

The table top is **flat**.
It is smooth and level.

The boys live in a **flat**.
All the rooms are on one floor.

float

The boat **floats** on the water.
It stays on top of the water.

flock

A group of sheep is a **flock**.

floor

The **floor** is the part of
a room we walk on.

flower

Many plants have
colourful **flowers**.
Here are some **flowers**.

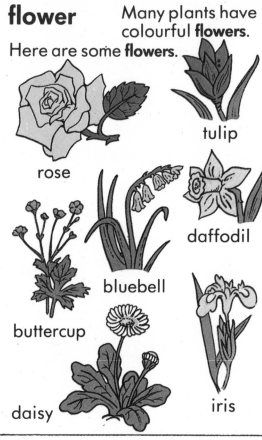

rose
tulip
daffodil
bluebell
buttercup
daisy
iris

fly

A **fly** is a small insect with wings.
It **flies** through the air.

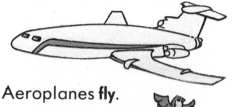

Aeroplanes **fly**.
So do most birds.

fog

Fog is very thick mist.

It is hard to see
in **foggy** weather.

follow

The little boy **follows**
his brother.
He walks behind him.

food

Food is all the things we eat.

bread
carrots
cheese
chicken
milk
icecream
potatoes
nuts
biscuits
spaghetti
pear

foot

The **foot** is at the
end of the leg.

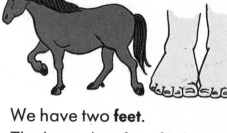

We have two **feet**.
The horse has four **feet**.

forest

A **forest** is a large
group of trees.

orget

on't **forget** to take your
ooks to school.

Don't leave them behind.

front   Fred is at the **front**
of the queue.

Fred's name is on the **front**
of his t-shirt.

funny   The clown is **funny**.

The clown makes the boy laugh.
Do you know any **funny** jokes?

our   **Four** tells us how many.

1   2

3   4

Four frogs.

fruit

A **fruit** is the part of a plant
or tree that holds the seeds.

The apple is the **fruit**
of the apple tree.

banana

blackberries

cherries

grapefruit

lemon

orange

melon

fur

The soft hairs on an animal's
body are its **fur**.

The polar bear has white **fur**.
The bear has brown **fur**.

furniture

Things in the rooms of a house
are called **furniture**.
All these things are **furniture**.

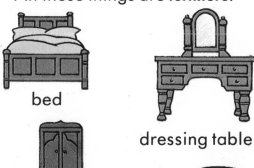

bed

dressing table

wardrobe

table

chest of drawers

chair

stool

sofa

desk

bookcase

lamp

ree   It doesn't cost anything
to get into the park.

It is **free**.

eeze   When something
freezes it turns to ice.

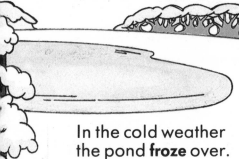

In the cold weather
the pond **froze** over.

iend

he children like each other.
hey are **friends**.

gooseberries

plum

fig

apricot

peach

g G

game

We play many **games**.

football

golf

marbles

cards

hide and seek

chess

dominoes

noughts and crosses

Games are fun.

gift

A **gift** is a present

David has brought Susan a **gift** for her birthday.

giraffe

The **giraffe** is the tallest animal in the world.

garage

A **garage** is a place where cars are kept.

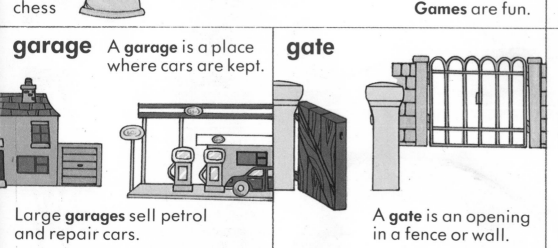

Large **garages** sell petrol and repair cars.

gate

A **gate** is an opening in a fence or wall.

glass

Glass is hard and clear. We can usually see through it.

Glasses help us see better.

garden

A **garden** is a piece of ground for growing things in.

get

How much pocket money do you **get**?

glove

Gloves are worn on the hands.

Gloves keep hands warm and

goat

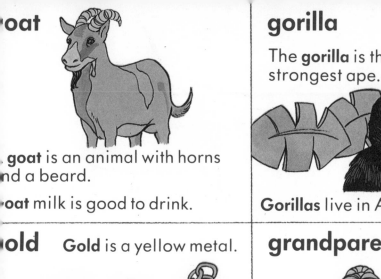

A **goat** is an animal with horns and a beard.

Goat milk is good to drink.

gorilla

The **gorilla** is the largest, strongest ape.

Gorillas live in Africa.

group

A **group** is a number of things.

A **group** of people.
A **group** of pictures.

gold

Gold is a yellow metal.

All these things are made of **gold**.

grandparents

Mummy and Daddy's parents are our **grandparents**.

grow

Grow means to get bigger.

The sunflower **grows** — and **grows** — and **grows**.

goldfish

Goldfish are gold coloured.

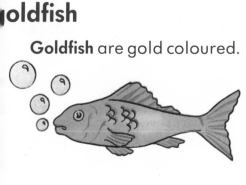

Goldfish are good pets.

grape

A **grape** is a small fruit.

Grapes grow in bunches.

growl

A **growl** is an angry sound made by a lion.

Dogs **growl**, too.

goodbye

Father is going away.

He waves **goodbye**.

grass

Grass is a plant with long, thin leaves.

guess

If we **guess** we are not really sure.

Can you **guess** what is in the parcel?

goose

A **goose** is a large bird with webbed feet and a long neck.
Geese are good swimmers.

green

Grass is **green**.

Leaves are **green**.

Apples are **green**.

guitar

A **guitar** is a musical instrument with strings.

h H

hair
Hair grows on your head.

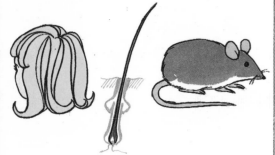

Animals have **hair**, too.

handle
A **handle** is something to hold.

The pan, the mug and the door all have **handles**.

hat
You wear a **hat** on yo[ur] hea[d]

Which **hat** do you like best?

half
The orange has been cut in **half**.

The two **halves** are exactly the same.

happy

When we are **happy** we are very pleased.

head

The **head** is the part of the bod[y] above the neck.

Head also means front or top. Hugh is at the **head** of the que[ue]

hand
You have two **hands**.

Hands hold, feel and pick things up.

Clocks have **hands**, too.

hard
Hard means solid, firm.
Hard means not soft.

Which of these things are **hard**?

Riding the bicycle is **hard**. It is not easy.

hear

What can you **hear** now?

We listen with our ears
We **hear** with our ears.

handkerchief

A **handkerchief** is a piece of cloth for wiping the nose. Hankie is another name for **handkerchief**.

Soft paper **handkerchieves** are called tissues.

heart

The **heart** pumps blood through our bodies.

Can you hear your **heart** beating?

heavy

Henry can't lift the suitcase.

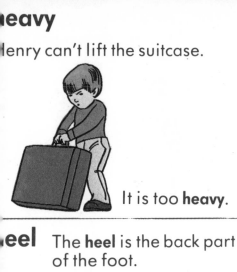

It is too **heavy**.

hen

A **hen** is a bird that lays eggs.

hole

The doughnut has a **hole** in it.

The sock has a **hole**, too.

heel

The **heel** is the back part of the foot.

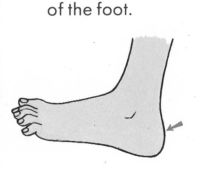

hide

The kitten is **hiding** under the table.

holiday

A **holiday** is a day when there is no work, no school. Christmas is a **holiday**.

Where do you go for your summer **holidays**?

helicopter

A **helicopter** is a machine that flies.

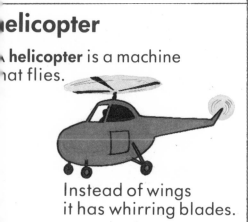

Instead of wings it has whirring blades.

hello

Hello is a greeting.

Hello is a friendly word.

high

High means far up.

The sun is **high** in the sky.

The building is **high**.

How **high** can you jump?

home

A **home** is a place to live.

Where is your **home**?

flats

houseboat

caravan

stone house

igloo

grass hut

Animals have **homes**, too.

kennel

nest

burrow

help

Helen is **helping** Mummy to wash the dishes.

To **help** is to do something for someone.

hill

A **hill** is a high piece of ground. How many **hills** can you see?

hop

Mary can jump on one leg.
She can **hop**.

hospital

A **hospital** is a place where
people go when they are ill.

how

How means in what wa
Harry is learning **how**
to play the piano.

How means what amount.
How old are you?

How means in what condition.
How are you feeling today?

horn

Some animals have **horns**.
Horns are hard.

A **horn** is a musical instrument.

A car **horn** makes
a warning sound.

hot

The soup is too warm to drink.
It's too **hot**.

hotel

A **hotel** is a building where
people eat and sleep when
they are away from home.

hungry

Spot is **hungry**.
He wants some foo

horse

A **horse** is a four-footed animal.
Some **horses** run races.

Some **horses** pull carts.

Many people ride **horses**.

hour

An **hour** is a measure of time.

There is an **hour** between
two o'clock and three o'clock.

house

A **house** is a building we live in.

hurry

When we
hurry
we do something quickly.

hurt

The boy has **hurt** his arm.
He has injured it.

i l

ce   **Ice** is frozen water.

e keeps food cold.

ill

Tom is **ill**. He is not well.

inside

The **inside** of the box is red.
The outside
is blue.

What is **inside** the box?

ecream

ecream is good to eat.
ecream is cold.

ink   **Ink** is coloured liquid.

We fill pens with **ink**
to write with.

invite

To **invite** is to ask to come.

Who are you going to **invite**
to your party?

I'm going to **invite**
the whole class!

icle

When it is very cold, running
ter may freeze and make **icicles**.

insect

An **insect** is a small animal
with six legs.

bee   flea

ladybird

dragonfly

beetle

moth   stick
insect

iron   Mummy uses an **iron**
to **iron** my dress.

It makes it smooth and flat.
    Iron is a hard metal.

island

An **island** is a piece of land
with water all around it.

dea

n **idea** is a thought or plan.
hat shall we play? Any **ideas**?
ve got a great **idea** —
t's play hide and seek!

j J

jacket

A **jacket** is a short coat.

job A **job** is something that people work at.

Teaching is a **job**.

Driving is a **job**.

jug A **jug** holds thing

juice

What is in the jug? Orange **juice**!

jam **Jam** is a sweet food made of fruit and sugar.

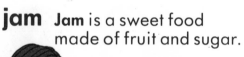

jar

The jam is in a glass **jar**.

joke

A **joke** makes people laugh.

Paul is going to play a **joke**.

jump

Jane **jumps** over the rop

jeans

Jeans are kinds of trousers.

journey

These people are going on a trip. They are going on a **journey**.

jungle

Can you see any wild animals in the **jungle**?

jelly A **jelly** is a cold, clear, fruity pudding.

A **jellyfish** is a water animal.

judge

Mrs Smith is **judging** the onions. She's deciding which are best.

just It is **just** two o'clock. It is exactly two o'cloc

k K

keep

Where do you **keep** your bike?

In the shed.

kiss

Karen gives her doll a **kiss**.

knee

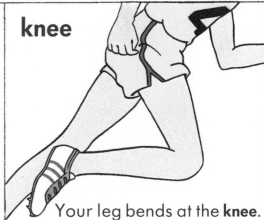

Your leg bends at the **knee**.

key

Keys open and shut locks.

kitchen

The **kitchen** is the room where food is cooked.

knife

A **knife** is used for cutting.

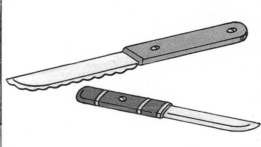

kick

Kevin **kicks** the football.

kite

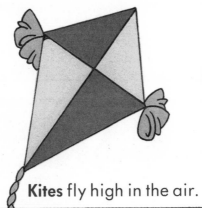

Kites fly high in the air.

knock

Keith **knocks** at the door.

Keith has **knocked** over the milk bottle.

kind

The boy is **kind** to his rabbit. He treats it well.

What **kind** of rabbit is it?
What sort of rabbit is it?

kitten

A **kitten** is a young cat.

This **kitten** is trying to catch the kite.

knot

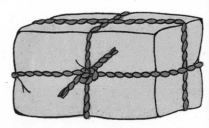

A **knot** ties things together.
There is a **knot** in the string.

l L

ladder

A **ladder** is a set of steps that can be moved around.

lazy

A **lazy** person is one who does not want to work.

left

Lenny holds up his **left** fo...

Linda holds up her **left** hand.

lamb

A **lamb** is a young sheep.

lead

The drummer **leads** the band. The drummer is at the front.

letter

There are 26 **letters** in the alphabet.

The postman puts a **letter** in the **letterbox**.

A **letter** is a message.

large

Large means big.

Pick out the **large** leaf.

leaf

Leaves grow on trees, plants and bushes.

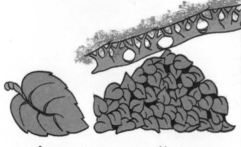

Leaves are usually green.

library

A **library** is a place where books are ke...

Do you borrow books from a **library**?

late

Laurence is **late** for school.

He is not on time.

leave

Shall I move the chair? No, **leave** it there.

I'm going to **leave** now. I'm going away.

lid

The pan's cover is called a **lid**.

Eyes have **lids**, too...

To **lie** means to rest flat.
The boy **lies** on the bed.

...e also means to say ...omething that isn't true.

like To **like** means to enjoy or be pleased by.

Do you **like** icecream?

Do you **like** to play?

lock

When things are **locked**, they cannot be opened without a key.
The door has a **lock**.

So does the box.

...ift The man **lifts** the box.

He moves it higher.

...ifts are machines that ...ove people up or down.

...all buildings have **lifts** ...nstead of stairs.

line The children form a **line**.
They make a row.

What colour is the **line**?
What colour is the thin mark?

look

Leo **looks** at the bird.
Lynn **looks**, too.

Larry **looks** in a mirror.

lip Your mouth has two **lips**.

Lips help you speak, sing — and whistle!

loud

The children make a **loud** noise.

It is easily heard.

...ight These things are **light**.

They are not heavy. They are easy to pick up.

...is **light** during the day.
...he electric bulb makes **light**.

...ne pair of jeans are dark blue.
...he other pair are **light** blue.

listen To **listen** is to hear.

The man is **listening** to music.

loaf A **loaf** is a piece of bread.

Can you see a brown **loaf**?

low

The bush is **low**.
It is near the ground.

Is the tree **low**?

lunch

Lunch is a meal eaten in the middle of the day.

m M

machine

A **machine** helps us to get work done.

Machines make jobs easier.

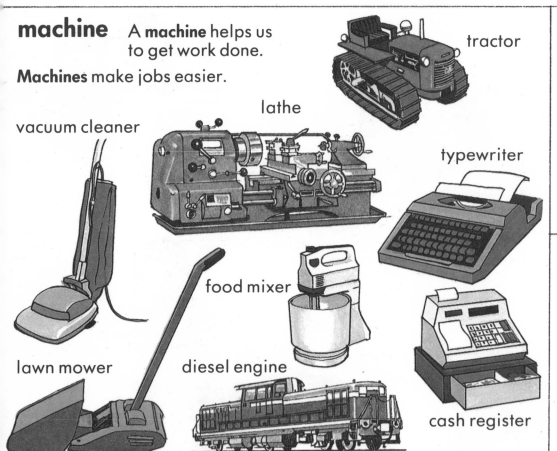

tractor

lathe

vacuum cleaner

typewriter

food mixer

lawn mower

diesel engine

cash register

map

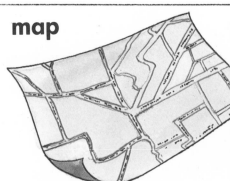

A **map** helps us find our way.
A **map** shows us where things

march

When we **march** we walk in lin
When we **march** we keep in st

magic

The man pulled scarves from a hat.

It was a trick. It was **magic**.

man

When he grows up the boy will be a **man**.

mark

There is a dirty mar
on Susan's dress.

The teacher **marks** David's su
She **marks** which are right —
and which are wrong.

The line **marks**
where the race starts.
On your **mark**, get set, GO!

make

Matt **makes** a castle.

Matt **makes** a cake.

many

There are **many** people watching football.

There are a lot of people.

How **many**?

market

A **market** is a busy place where things are bought and sold.

meet

The ladies **meet** at the market every week. They go to see each other.

mirror

You can see yourself in a **mirror**. **Mirrors** are made of glass.

mat

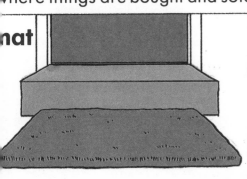

A **mat** is a small rug.

melt

When ice and snow **melt** they change to water.

miss

David **missed** the target. He failed to hit the target.

Susan **missed** the bus. It went without her.

match

Mary's hat, gloves and scarf **match**. They are all the same colour.

Mummy uses a **match** to light the fire.

Let's watch the tennis **match**. A **match** is a game, or contest.

middle

There is a white line in the **middle** of the road. It is in the centre.

The triangle is in the **middle** of the circles.

milk

Milk comes from cows. **Milk** is good to drink.

mistake

Mike put salt in his tea. It was a **mistake**. He didn't mean to do it.

measure

To **measure** is to find the size or amount of something.

Mummy **measures** out some milk.

Daddy **measures** a piece of wood.

minute

A **minute** is a measure of time. There are 60 seconds in a **minute**. There are 60 **minutes** in an hour.

mix

To **mix** means to put together. Mummy **mixes** a cake **mix**.

money

Money is used to buy things.

Money is coins.

Money is banknotes.

moon

The **moon** shines in the night sky.

The **moon** changes shape.

mouth

We use our **mout**
to eat and talk.

more

Mark wants **more** pie.

He wants another piece.

move

Move means to go
to another place.

The train **moves**
out of the station.
Move means to put
somewhere else.

The dog **moves** his bon
to a new hole.

monkey

A **monkey** is
a tree-climbing animal.

morning

Morning is the first
part of the day.

much

How **much** is it to New Road?
What does it cost?

month

A **month** is part of a year.
There are twelve **months** in a year.
Can you name them?

January	February	March
April	May	June
July	August	September
October	November	December

mountain

A **mountain** is a very high
piece of land.

Which is higher —
a **mountain** or a hill?

music

Music is pleasing sounds mad
by instruments or voices.

mouse

A **mouse** is a small furry anima
with a long tail.

Mice make good pets.

musical instruments

violin

piano

cello

recorder

n N

9 9 9 9 9 9 9 9 9 9 9 9 9 9 9 9 9 9 9 9

nail

Metal **nails** hold things together.

We have **nails** in our fingers and toes.

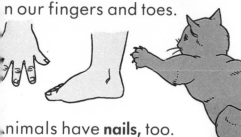

Animals have **nails,** too. They are called claws.

near

The dog sits **near** his owner. He sits close to his owner.

nearly

Number 5 **nearly** won the race. He almost won.

neighbour

Neighbours live near each other. The two boys are **neighbours.**

neither

Which bun would you like? **Neither**, I don't like buns.

Neither means not one or the other.

name

DAVID   SUSAN

Our **name** is what we are called. Our **name** is what we are known as.

What is your **name**?

neck   Nancy's **neck** is short.

The giraffe's **neck** is long.

nest   A bird's home is a **nest.**

Ants live in **nests**, too.

narrow

The gap in the fence is **narrow.** It is not wide.

need

Need means must have.

Ned **needs** a bath.

never   **Never** means not ever.

Never cross the road without looking both ways.

new The blue car is **new**.

The green car isn't **new**.
It's very old.

news

The **news** tells us
what has been happening.

newspaper

We read the news
in a **newspaper**.

next

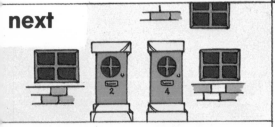

Next means nearest to.
The houses are **next** to each other.

a b c d

What is the **next** letter after d?
The **next** letter is e.

Next, please!

night It is dark at **night**.

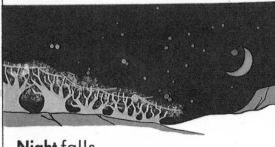

Night falls
when the sun goes down.

nine **Nine** tells us how many.

Here are **nine nines**!

9	9	9
9	9	9
9	9	9

nobody

Who is in the classroom?

4×7=

Nobody! It's empty.

noise **Noises** are sounds.

The dog's bark is a **noise**.

The car's horn makes a **noise**.

none **None** means not one.

None of the children
have blond hair.
Not one has blond hair

nose We breathe and smel
through our **noses**.

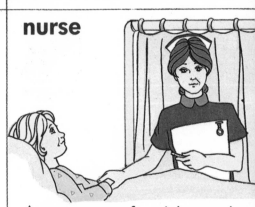

The dog smells
with his **nose**, too.

number

A **number** tells us how many.

Do you know the **numbers**
from 1 to 20?

1	2	3	4
5	6	7	8
9	10	11	12
13	14	15	16
17	18	19	20

nurse

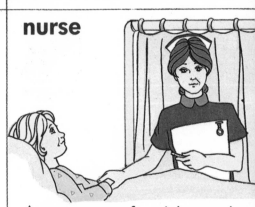

A **nurse** cares for sick people.

nut **Nuts** are the seeds of
some plants and trees.

peanut

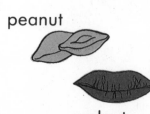

hazelnut

walnut

Nuts have hard shells.

o O

ak The **oak** is a large tree.

s fruit is the acorn.

office

An **office** is where people work.

once

Once means at one time.

Dinosaurs **once** lived on earth.

cean

n **ocean** is a large sea.

Do you know the names of any **oceans**?

oil **Oil** is liquid grease.

Daddy puts **oil** in his car engine. It helps it to run smoothly.

one **One** tells us how many.

Oliver has **one** white glove and **one** black.

dd Which is the **odd** sock?

hich sock is different om the rest?

Mummy uses cooking **oil**. She fries food in it.

only

Only one of the sweets is red.

ff **Off** means not on.

avid turned the radio **off**.

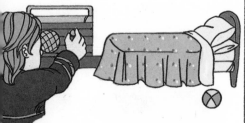

The ball rolled **off** the bed.

old The train is **old**. It is not new.

How **old** are you?

open The window is **open**.

The door is **open**.

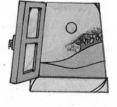

They are not closed.

orange

An **orange** is a fruit.

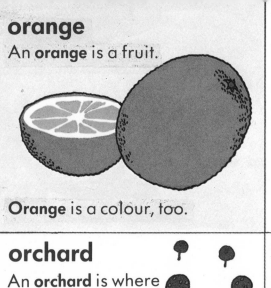

Orange is a colour, too.

other

I don't like this hat. Have you any **others**?

Have you any different ones?

over

Jane holds the umbrella **over** her head.

When will this programme be **over**? When will it finish?

How many nails are there? **Over** twenty. More than twenty.

orchard

An **orchard** is where fruit trees grow.

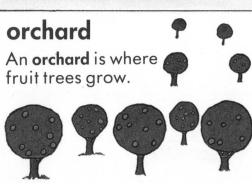

What is growing in this **orchard**? Oranges!

out

David and Susan look **out** of the window.

"Shall we go **out**?" says David.

order

An **order** is a command.

The officer shouts **orders**, and the soldiers obey.

a b c d e f g

The letters are in alphabetical **order**.

We don't have your size, but we can **order** it.

outdoors

David is going **outdoors**.

Susan is **outdoors** already.

overalls

Oliver wears **overalls** to paint. They cover him all over.

outside

David and Susan are **outside** the house.

They are not inside.

owl

An **owl** is a bird with large eye

organ

Organs make music.

Organs are in most churches.

oven

What is baking in the **oven**?

It's a pie!

own

The girl has a puppy of her ow It belongs to her.

Say some things that you own

p P

page Books and newspapers have **pages**.

How many **pages** in this book?

pain Peter is in **pain**. His knee hurts.

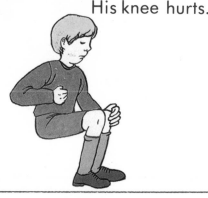

paint Pat **paints** a picture.

Daddy **paints** the shed. What colour is the **paint**?

pair A **pair** means two things that match.

Can you see a **pair** of mittens?

palm The inside of your hand is called the **palm**.

A **palm** is a tall tree. It grows in warm lands.

paper

We write and draw on **paper**. We read from **paper**. We hang **paper** on walls. We wrap things in **paper**.

parcel A **parcel** is a small package.

What is the **parcel** wrapped in? Paper!

parent

A **parent** is a father or mother. Mummy is a **parent**.

Daddy is a **parent**.

park

A **park** is an open space, with grass, trees and flowers.

Some **parks** have a playground, too.

party

Friends have fun together at a **party**.

Whose **party** do you think it is?

pavement

A **pavement** is a path beside the road, for people to walk on.

pay

I'll **pay** for your ticket. I'll give the money for it.

pen

A **pen** writes with ink.

pencil

We write with **pencils**, too.

people

Human beings are **people**.

Men and women, boys and girls are **people**.

We are all **people**.

pet

A **pet** is an animal that we feed and take care of.

Do you have a **pet**?

goldfish

mouse

dog

canary

rabbit

cat

hamster

picnic

At **picnics** we eat outdoors.

picture

A **picture** is a drawing, painting or photograph.

There are **pictures** on this page.

piece

The cake has been cut into **pieces**.

One **piece** is missing

pile

Paula swept the leaves into a **pile**.

pin

Pins fasten things.

Can you name these **pin**

plant

Trees, flowers, bushes and grasses are all **plants**.

Daddy is **planti** some bulbs.

He is putting them in the ground.

late

e eat food from a **plate**.

pocket

What does Peter have in his **pocket**?

A puppy!

pull

The children **pull** hard on the rope. They draw it towards them.

lay

play is a ow.

This is the school **play**.

e children **play** a game **play**time.

Pete **plays** a guitar.

pond

A **pond** is a small pool of water.

pony

A **pony** is a small horse.

puppet

Puppets are dolls that move.

A hand moves one **puppet**. Strings move the other **puppet**.

push

Mummy **pushes** a pram.

ayground

A **playground** is a special place to play.

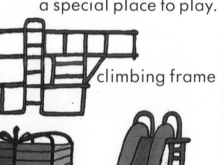

climbing frame

slide

undabout

seesaw

swings

post

Pete **posts** a letter. He sends it. The **postman** delivers the letter.

Have you been to a **post office**?

prize

A **prize** is something you get for winning or doing well.

Paul's picture won a **prize**.

put

David **puts** his sock on.

Daddy **puts** the teapot on the table.

puzzle

Pam is doing a jigsaw **puzzle**.

She doesn't know where the pieces go.

She is **puzzled**.

q Q

QUEUE HERE

quack

Quack is the noise a duck makes.

question

The teacher asks a **question**.

"What is today's date?"

The children answer her **question**.

quiet

Quiet, don't make a noise, the baby's sleeping.

quantity

Quantity is the amount or size of something.

Daddy ordered a large **quantity** of bricks.

queue

The children **queue** at the bus stop.

BUS STOP

They stand in line, one behind the other.

quilt

A **quilt** is a warm, thick bed cover.

quarrel

The children both want the book.

They are angry. They are **quarrelling**.

quite

Susan isn't **quite** as tall as Dav
She is nearly as tall.

quarter

To **quarter** is to cut into four equal parts.

A **quarter** is one of four equal parts.

quick

Quick means very fast.

Susan runs **quickly**.

quiz

A **quiz** is a test.

People doing a **quiz** have to answer questions.

r R

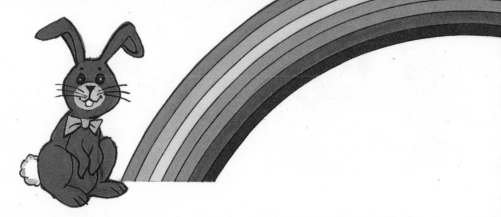

race The fastest runner will win the **race**.

Cars and horses **race**, too.

reach

Roy cannot **reach** the lemonade. He cannot touch it.

rest

One ball is green. All the **rest** are blue.

All the others are blue.

rain

rain is drops of water which fall from the clouds.

Do you like **rainy** weather?

real

Which is the **real** rabbit? Which is the toy rabbit?

Robin is tired. He **rests** on his bed.

rainbow

When sun shines through rain we see a **rainbow**.

A **rainbow** is a band of colour.

red **Red** is a colour.

All these things are **red**.

riddle

A **riddle** is a word puzzle. Here's a **riddle**.

What is black and white and read all over?

A newspaper!

raw **Raw** means not cooked.

Which foods do we eat **raw**?

remember

Can you **remember** what you got for Christmas?

Can you think back?

ride To **ride** is to go somewhere on something. We **ride** on bicycles.

We **ride** on buses.

We **ride** on horses.

right

Tom holds up his **right** hand.
Hold up your **right** hand.

Tom got his sum **right**.
His sum is correct.

ring

Do you wear a **ring** on your finger?

The circus **ring** is round.

Roy **rings** the doorbell.

river

A **river** is a large stream of water.

road

Cars and buses travel on **roads**.

We cross the **road** at crossings.

rock

Rock is stone.

Grandma **rocks**
in her rocking chair.

roll

A **roll** is a small piece of bread.

The man **rolls** up the carpet.

The marbles **roll** across the floor.
So does David!

roof

A **roof** covers the top of buildings.

room

Rooms are different
parts of the house.

This is David's **room**.

rough

The sea is **rough**. It is not smoo

How does an egg feel?
Smooth or **rough**?

round

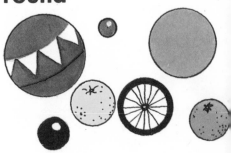

All these things are roun

row

The flowers are planted in a r
They are in a line.

The man **rows** a **row**ing boat.
He uses wooden oars.

run   To **run** is to move quick

The man and the dog **run** quic
The stream **runs**, too.

s S

---

ack A **sack** is a large bag.

The children are in a **sack** race.

---

scare To **scare** means to frighten.

Sam is trying to **scare** his sister.
She doesn't look **scared**, does she?

---

sea The **sea** is a very big area of salt water.

The **seaside** is beside the **sea**.

---

ame

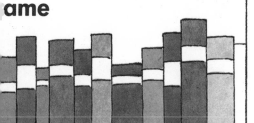

Which two books are the **same**?
Which two are alike?

---

and

and is very tiny pieces of rock.

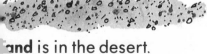

and is in the desert.

and is on the beach.

---

school

We go to **school** to learn.

Do you go to **school**?

---

season

There are four **seasons** in a year.

spring

summer

autumn

winter

---

ave To **save** is to keep something.

Sue **saves** her money.
She is **saving** to buy a doll.

---

scissors **Scissors** are two sharp blades.

Scissors cut paper, cloth — and hair!

---

seat

A **seat** is something to sit on.

A chair is a **seat**.

So is a stool.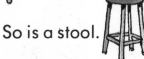

seed

Plants grow from **seeds**. The tall sunflower grew from the tiny **seed**.

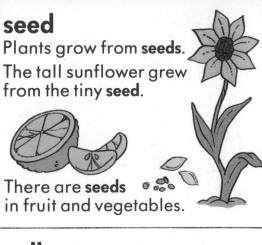

There are **seeds** in fruit and vegetables.

sell

To **sell** is to give things for money.

This shop **sells** fish.

shape

Shape is the form things take. Here are some different **shapes**.

round

square

rectangle

triangle

What **shape** is the sun?

shoe

Shoes cover feet.

What do you wear under shoe

Horses wear **shoes**, too — horse**shoes**.

shop

A **shop** is where we g to buy things.

What is sold in the blue **shop**?

Can you see the **shopkeep**

sense

To **sense** means to feel. We **sense** that the air is cold.

Our **senses** help us to see, hear, smell, taste and touch.

sheep

A **sheep** is an animal.

A **sheep** has hair called wool.

We make clothes from the wool of **sheep**,

shell

A **shell** is an outside cover.

Animals have **shells**.

tortoise

snail

Nuts have **shells**.

Eggs have **shells**.

shut

Shut means to close or fasten.

The door and the window are s Is the cupboard **shut**?

sing

When we **sing**, we make music with our voice The children **sing**.

Birds **sing**, too.

seven

Seven tells us how many.

1 2 3 4 5

6 7

ship

A **ship** is a very large boat.

six

Six tells us how many.

How many soldiers? **Six!**

size Size tells us how big or small things are.

What **size** are your shoes?

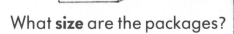

What **size** are the packages?

sleep
When we **sleep** we rest our body and mind.

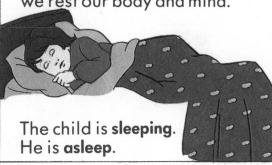

The child is **sleeping**. He is **asleep**.

snow
When rain freezes it turns to **snow**. **Snowflakes** fall from the air.

The children build a **snowman**. They throw **snowballs**.

smile
We **smile** when we are happy.

soap

Soap helps us clean things.

We wash our bodies with **soap**. We wash clothes with **soap** powder.

skate
Can you **skate**?

One child wears ice **skates**. The other wears roller **skates**.

smoke

Smoke comes from fires.

soft
Soft means not hard, not loud.

David's pillow is **soft**.

Mummy speaks in a **soft** voice.

skin
Our body is covered in **skin**.

An apple is covered in **skin**, too.

smooth

Smooth means flat, without any bumps.

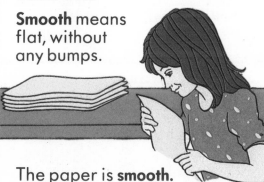

The paper is **smooth**.

sound We hear **sounds**.

Sound is noise.

sky The **sky** is the space above the earth.

Sometimes the **sky** is blue.

Sometimes the **sky** is grey. What colour is the **sky** today?

snake
A **snake** is a long thin animal.

Snakes have no legs. Do you think **snakes** are smooth?

speak

The teacher **speaks** to the class. She talks to them.

stairs
Stairs are steps.

We go up**stairs** and come down**stairs**.

stick
A **stick** is a small piece of wood.
Stan hit the stone with a **stick**.

We **stick** things together with glue.

street

A **street** is a small road in a town or city.

stamp
A **stamp** shows you have paid to send a letter.

Some people collect **stamps** from different countries.

Sue is angry. She **stamps** her foot.

stop
Stop means to finish or halt.

The bus **stops** at a bus **stop**.

strong

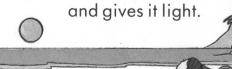

The man is **strong**. He can lift heavy things.

star
We see **stars** in the sky at night.

Can you count all the **stars**?

Sarah draws a **star** shape.

storm
In a **storm** it rains hard and the wind blows.

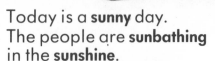

In **stormy** weather we may see thunder and lightning, too.

sun
The **sun** warms the ear and gives it light.

Today is a **sunny** day. The people are **sunbathing** in the **sunshine**.

start
To **start** means to begin.
The runners wait for the race to **start**.

What time does the play **start**?

story
A **story** is a tale.
We tell **stories**.
We read **stories**, too.

Which **stories** are these?

sweep

Mary **sweeps** up leaves and li
She brushes them into a pile.

stay
To **stay** means to stop or wait.

The boy tells the dog to **stay**.
He tells him not to move.

swim
Mary can **swim**.
She uses her arms and legs to move through the water.

Do you like **swimming**
Are you a **swimmer**?

t T

table

Tables are flat pieces of furniture with legs.

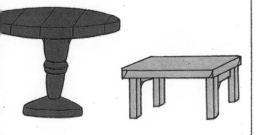

What are these **tables** for?

taste

When we eat things we **taste** them.

Sweets **taste** sweet.

Lemons **taste** sour.

television

A **television** brings pictures and sounds into our homes.

Television is called TV, too.

tail

These animals all have **tails**.

The kite has a **tail** too.

taxi

A **taxi** is a car that people pay to ride in.

ten

Ten tells us how many.

Here are **ten** tents.

tall

Tall means very high.

This tree is the **tallest**.

This tree is **taller**.

The tree is **tall**.

tea

Tea is a drink.

Tom pours **tea** from a **teapot**.

It is **teatime**.

telephone

A **telephone** carries sounds from one person to another.

With a **telephone** we can speak to people far away.

tent

People sleep outdoors in **tents**.

People camp in **tents**.

thick

The book is **thick**. It has lots of pages.

Toms wears a **thick** jumper. It keeps him warm.

thin
Thin means not wide or fat.

A sheet of paper is **thin**.

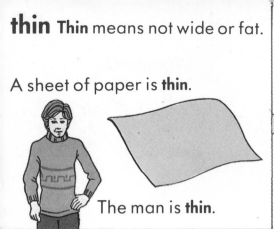

The man is **thin**.

ticket
A **ticket** is a piece of paper that shows we have paid.

You need **tickets** to travel on trains and buses.

together
Together means with someone or something

The children are all playing **together**.
The cat and dog are sitting **together**.

thirsty
When we have a **thirst** we want to drink.

Tom and Tim are **thirsty**.

tie
To **tie** means to join together.

Tim **ties** up the parcel.

Daddy wears a **tie** around his neck.

tongue
Your **tongue** helps you to taste.
Your **tongue** helps you to talk.

The snake has a long **tong**

three
Three tells us how many.

Here are **three** tigers.

time
Time tells us what part of the day it is.

Can you tell the **time**?

Clocks and watches tell us the **time**.

Eight o'clock. **Time** to get up.

Half past seven. **Time** to go to sleep.

What **time** is it now?

tool
Tools help make work easier.

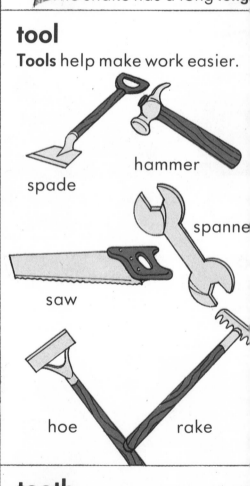

spade

hammer

spanne

saw

hoe

rake

thumb
On each hand you have four fingers and a **thumb**.

Thumbs help us grip and lift things.

thunder
Thunder is a loud noise.

In storms we often hear **thunder** and see lightning.

toe

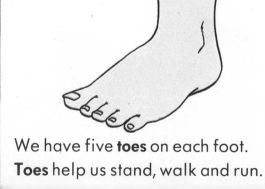

We have five **toes** on each foot.
Toes help us stand, walk and run.

tooth
Teeth help us talk and eat.

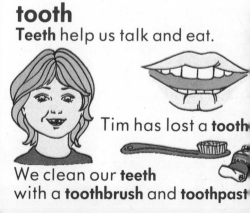

Tim has lost a **tooth**

We clean our **teeth** with a **toothbrush** and **toothpast**

op

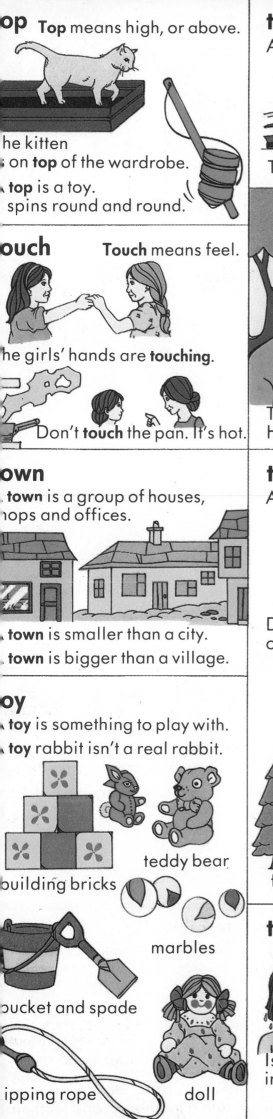

Top means high, or above.

he kitten
s on **top** of the wardrobe.

top is a toy.
spins round and round.

ouch

Touch means feel.

he girls' hands are **touching**.

Don't **touch** the pan. It's hot.

own

town is a group of houses,
 hops and offices.

town is smaller than a city.
town is bigger than a village.

oy

toy is something to play with.

toy rabbit isn't a real rabbit.

teddy bear

building bricks

marbles

bucket and spade

ipping rope   doll

train

A **train** carries people and goods.

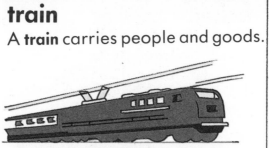

The **train** is pulled by an engine.

Terry **trains** his dog.
He shows him what to do.

tree

A **tree** is a very big plant.

Do you know the names
of these **trees**?

oak

ash

beech

fir   willow   chestnut

true

When something is **true**
it really happened.

Is it **true** that you fell
in a puddle? Yes, it's **true**.

The boy is telling the **truth**.

twelve

Twelve tells us how many.

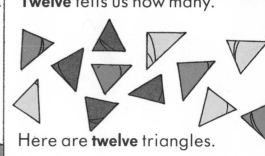

Here are **twelve** triangles.
Dozen is another word for **twelve**.

twin

Twins are two children
born on the same day.

Twins have the same
Mummy and Daddy.

Some **twins** look alike.

two

Two tells us how many.

Here are **two** turtles.
And **two** tricycles.

typewriter

A **typewriter** is a writing machine.

A **typist** uses a **typewriter**.

tyre

Cars and bicycles run on **tyres**.

The car needs a new **tyre**.

The bicycle **tyre** needs more air.

u U

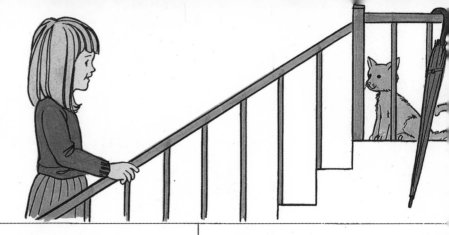

umbrella

An **umbrella** keeps off rain.
An **umbrella** keeps us dry.

underwear

Underwear are things we wear
under our outer clothes.

upstairs

Upstairs means
the top of the stairs.

Daddy is walking **upstairs**.
Spot is **upstairs** already.

under

Under means below, beneath.

The hat is **under** the chair.
The mouse is **under** the hat.

uniform

The children wear school **uniform**.
They wear the same clothes.

The policeman
wears a **uniform**, too.

use

Use means to do something wit

Do you know how
to **use** a camera?
Mary has **used** one before.

underground

Underground means under
the ground.

Many things are **underground**.

up

Up means higher, above,
away from the ground.

The aeroplane flies **up**
into the sky.

String has many **uses**.
We can do lots of things with it

understand

To **understand** is to know

Mary **understands** the recipe.
She knows what it means.

upside-down

Upside-down means
turned the wrong way.

The boy is hanging **upside-down**.
The bucket is **upside-down**.

useful

Tools are **useful**.
They help us build things.

Books are **useful**.
They help us learn things.
Useful is anything that is of use

v V

valley

A **valley** is the land between two hills.

The river runs along the **valley**.

value

Value means worth. What is the **value** of the bike?

What is its price? What is it worth? Is the bike **valuable**?

van

A **van** is a kind of car used for carrying things.

What is this **van** carrying?

vase

A **vase** is made to hold flowers.

vegetable

Vegetables are parts of plants we eat as food.

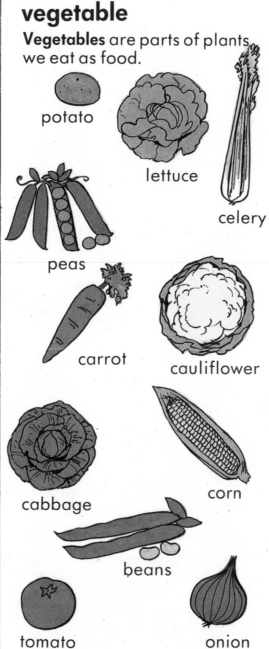

potato

lettuce

celery

peas

carrot

cauliflower

corn

cabbage

beans

tomato

onion

village

A **village** is a small town.

violin

Violins make music.

A **violin** has four strings. It is played with a bow.

visit

Visit means to go and see.

Do you **visit** your grandparents?

Do you **visit** the library?

voice

When we speak we use our **voices**.

When we sing we use our **voices**. Our **voice** is the noise we make.

volcano

A **volcano** is a mountain with a hole in the top.

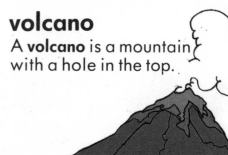

Melted rock and steam pour from some **volcanoes**.

w W

wait

wait To **wait** means to stay. I've forgotten my books. Will you **wait** for me?

Yes, but hurry, I'm not **waiting** long.

watch

watch **Watch** means look.

William **watches** television.

What is the cat **watching**?

A **watch** tells the time.

week

week A **week** is seven days.

There are 52 **weeks** in a year.

Do you know the days of the week?

Monday
Tuesday
Wednesday
Thursday
Friday
Saturday
Sunday

Weekend means Saturday and Sunday.

walk

walk To **walk** is to move on foot.

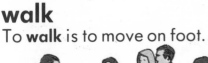

The people are all **walking**. Wayne takes his dog for a **walk**.

water

water

Water is liquid.
Water is rain.
We drink **water**.
Plants drink **water**.

Water is in ponds, rivers and the sea.

wall

wall

The side of a building is a **wall**. A brick or stone fence is a **wall**.

weather

weather
Weather is how wet, dry, hot or cold it is outside.

What kind of **weather** are you having today?

windy   sunny

snowy   rainy

What kind of **weather** do you like best?

weigh

weigh **Weigh** means find out how heavy something is

The boy is being **weighed**.

The man **weighs** some sweets.

wash

wash When we **wash** things we clean them.

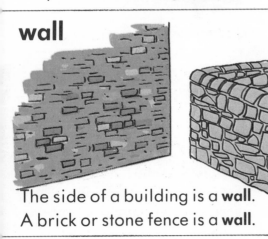

Wendy **washes** her hands. What is Daddy **washing**

wet

wet **Wet** means covered with water.

When it rains it is a **wet** day. Mummy hangs out the **wet** washing.

whale

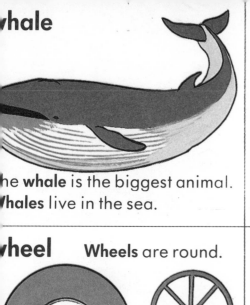

The **whale** is the biggest animal.
Whales live in the sea.

whole

Whole means all.
The boy ate a **whole** apple.

work

Work is something to do.

Work is a job.
Mummy **works** in the garden.
What **work** are these people doing?

wheel

Wheels are round.

Wheels help things move.
Mummy **wheels** the pram.

win

To **win** means to come first.

William **wins** the race.
He is the **winner**.

window

Windows let in air and light.
Wendy waves from her **window**.

world

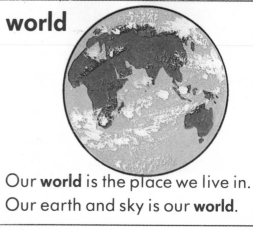

Our **world** is the place we live in.
Our earth and sky is our **world**.

whisper

Whisper means speak very quietly.
Wendy is **whispering**.

wing

Wings help things fly.

write

When we **write** we put words on paper.

Jane is **writing** her name.
Peter is **writing** his address.

white

White is a colour.

How many **white** things can you see?

woman

A **woman** is a grown-up.

Mummy is a **woman**.
Susie is a girl.
She will grow up to be a **woman**.

wrong

Wrong means not correct.
David got his sum **wrong**.

Wrong means not good, not right.
It is **wrong** to tell lies.

x X

y Y

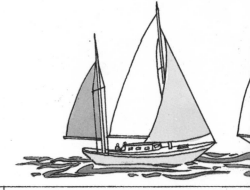

Xmas

Xmas is another way of writing Christmas.

yacht

A **yacht** is a small boat with sails.

yell

A **yell** is a loud shout

yawn

We **yawn** when we feel sleepy.

We open our mouths wide and take a big breath.

yellow

Yellow is a colour.

All these things are **yellow.**

x-ray

X-rays take pictures of the insides of our bodies.

The doctor **x-rayed** Paul's arm to see if it was broken.

year

A **year** is a measure of time.

There are 12 months in a **year.**

There are 365 days in a **year,** but 366 in a special leap **year.**

yes

When we say **yes** we agree.
Will you come to my party?
Yes!

yesterday

Yesterday is the day before today

If today is Tuesday, **yesterday** was Monday.

xylophone

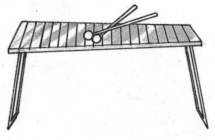

A **xylophone** makes music.

What **year** were you born?
What **year** is it now?

z Z

olk

The **yolk** is the yellow part of an egg.

zebra

A **zebra** is a striped animal.

It is like a small horse.

zoo

A **zoo** is a place where wild animals and birds are kept.

rhinoceros

chimpanzee

tiger

toucan

penguin

llama

antelope

sea lion

elephant

oung

oung means not grown up.

A puppy is a **young** dog.

A **young** cat is a kitten.

zero

Zero tells us how many.

Zero means none at all.

our

Anything that is **yours** belongs to you.

Touch **your** head.

Clap **your** hands.

zigzag

Zigzag means to move from side to side.

The path **zigzags** through the park.

o-yo

A **yo-yo** is a toy.

zip

A **zip** fastens things together.

Zoe **zips** up her anorak.